Black Sabbath
for ukulele

Eighteen classic Black Sabbath rockers arranged for ukulele!
Complete with full lyrics, chord boxes, and all your favorite riffs in tablature!

HAL•LEONARD®

Cover photo: Chris Walter/Getty Images
Project editor: David Bradley
Arrangements for publication by Martin Shellard

Order No. AM1001616
International Standard Book Number: 978-0-8256-3754-4
HL Item Number: 14037748

Exclusive Distributors:

Hal Leonard
7777 West Bluemound Road, Milwaukee, WI 53213 Email: info@halleonard.com

Hal Leonard Europe Limited
42 Wigmore Street, Marylebone, London WIU 2 RY Email: info@halleonardeurope.com

Hal Leonard Australia Pty. Ltd. 4 Lentara Court, Cheltenham, Victoria 9132, Australia
Email: info@halleonard.com.au

Printed in EU.

www.halleonard.com

CHILDREN OF THE GRAVE

**Words and Music by Frank Iommi, William Ward,
John Osbourne and Terence Butler**

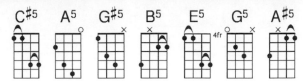

Moderately fast

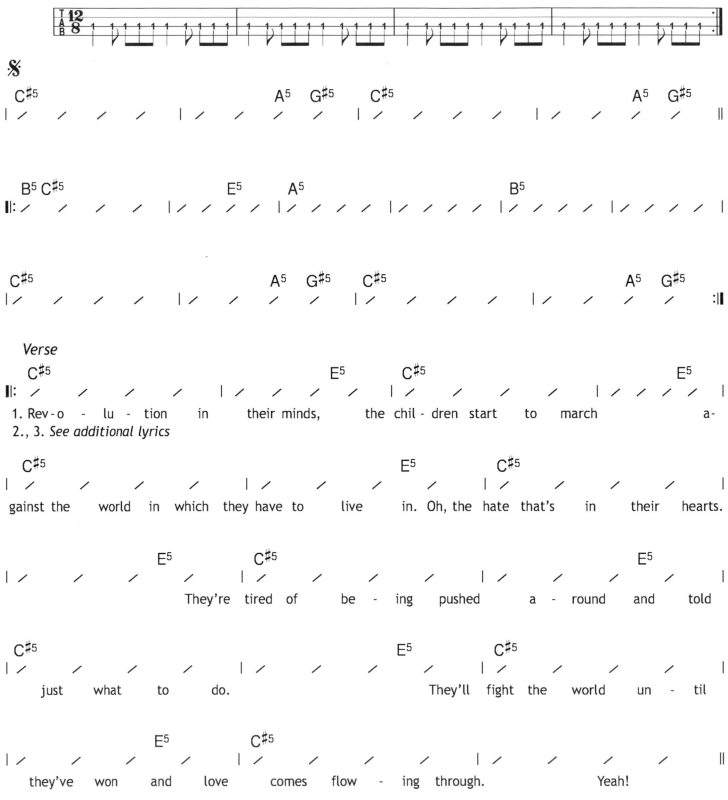

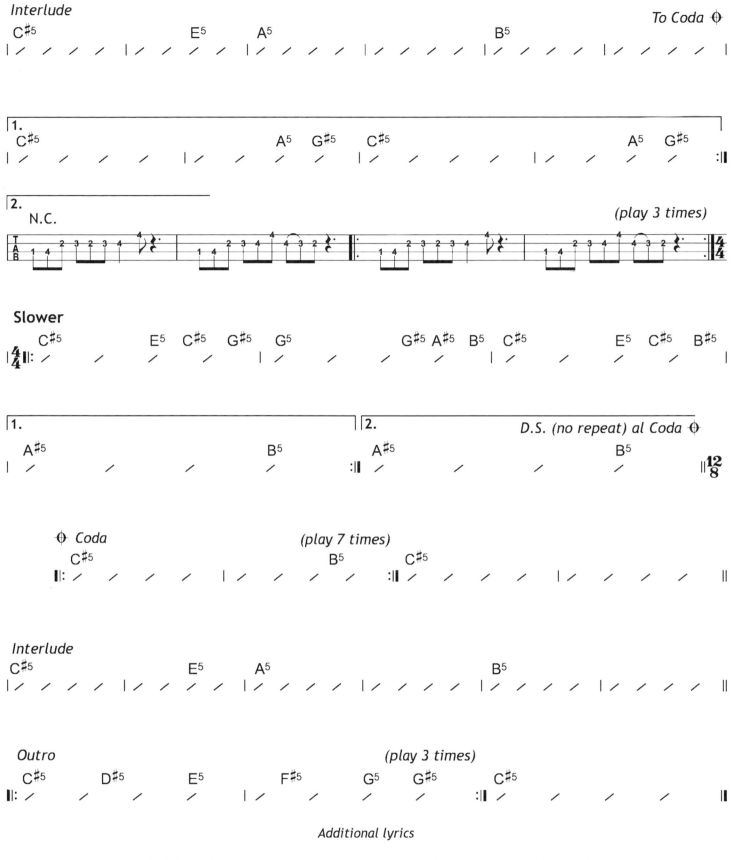

Additional lyrics

2. Children of tomorrow live
   In the tears that fall today.
   Will the sunrise of tomorrow
   Bring in peace in any way?
   Must the world live in the shadow
   Of atomic fear?
   Can they win the fight for peace
   Or will they disappear?
   Yeah!

3. So you children of the world,
   Listen to what I say.
   If you want a better place to live in,
   Then spread the word today.
   Show the world that love is still alive,
   You must be brave,
   Or you children of today
   Are children of the grave.
   Yeah!

DIRTY WOMEN

**Words and Music by Frank Iommi, John Osbourne,
William Ward and Terence Butler**

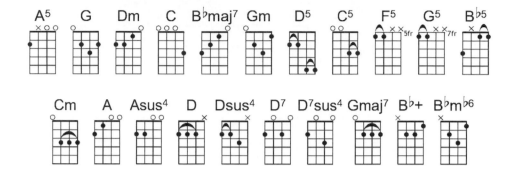

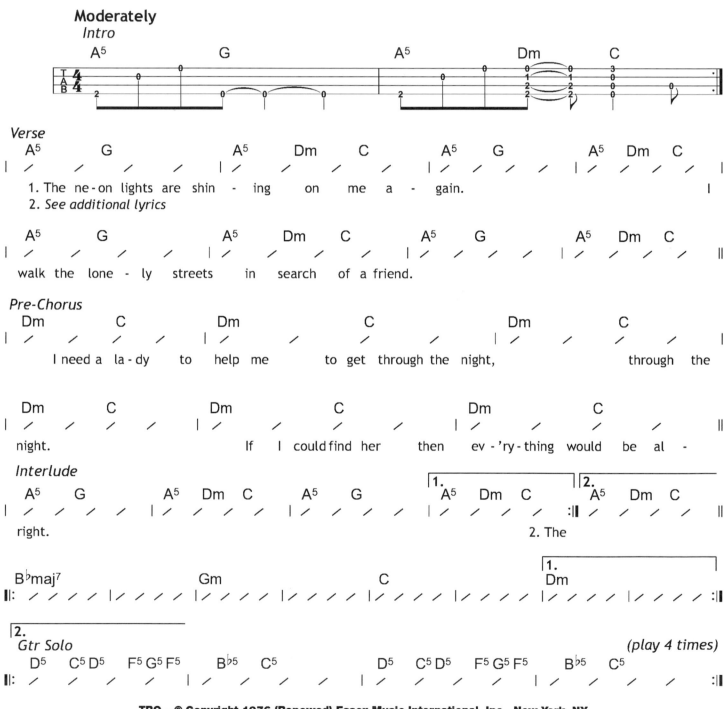

Moderately

Intro

Verse

1. The ne-on lights are shin - ing on me a - gain.
2. *See additional lyrics*

walk the lone - ly streets in search of a friend.

Pre-Chorus

I need a la - dy to help me to get through the night, through the

night. If I could find her then ev - 'ry-thing would be al -

Interlude

right. 2. The

Gtr Solo (play 4 times)

B♭maj⁷　　　　　　Gm　　　　　　C　　　　　　**1.** Dm

‖: ╱ ╱ ╱ ╱ | ╱ ╱ ╱ ╱ | ╱ ╱ ╱ ╱ | ╱ ╱ ╱ ╱ | ╱ ╱ ╱ ╱ | ╱ ╱ ╱ ╱ | ╱ ╱ ╱ ╱ | ╱ ╱ ╱ ╱ :‖

2. Dm　　　　　　Cm　　　　　*(play 4 times)*　Asus⁴ A　　Asus⁴ A　　Asus⁴ A　　G

‖: ╱ ╱ ╱ ╱ | ╱ ╱ ╱ ╱ :‖ ╱ ╱ ╱ ╱ | ╱ ╱ ╱ ╱ | ╱ ╱ ╱ ╱ | ╱ ╱ ╱ ╱ |

D⁵　C⁵ D⁵　F⁵ G⁵ F⁵　B♭⁵　C⁵　　　　　D⁵　C⁵ D⁵　F⁵ G⁵ F⁵　B♭⁵　C⁵

| ╱ ╱ ╱ ╱ | ╱ ╱ ╱ ╱ | ╱ ╱ ╱ ╱ | ╱ ╱ ╱ ╱ ‖

　　　　　　　　　　　　　　　　　　　　　Oh, dirt - y

Chorus

D⁵　C⁵ D⁵　F⁵ G⁵ F⁵　B♭⁵　　C⁵　　　　D⁵　C⁵ D⁵　F⁵ G⁵ F⁵　B♭⁵　C⁵

| ╱ ╱ ╱ ╱ | ╱ ╱ ╱ ╱ | ╱ ╱ ╱ ╱ | ╱ ╱ ╱ ╱ |

wom - en,　　　they　don't mess a - round.　　　　　Oh, dirt - y

D⁵　C⁵ D⁵　F⁵ G⁵ F⁵　B♭⁵　　C⁵　　　　D⁵　C⁵ D⁵　F⁵ G⁵ F⁵　B♭⁵　C⁵

| ╱ ╱ ╱ ╱ | ╱ ╱ ╱ ╱ | ╱ ╱ ╱ ╱ | ╱ ╱ ╱ ╱ |

wom - en,　　　they　don't mess a - round.　　　　You've got　me

D⁵　C⁵ D⁵　F⁵ G⁵ F⁵　B♭⁵　　C⁵　　　　D⁵　C⁵ D⁵　F⁵ G⁵ F⁵　B♭⁵　C⁵

| ╱ ╱ ╱ ╱ | ╱ ╱ ╱ ╱ | ╱ ╱ ╱ ╱ | ╱ ╱ ╱ ╱ |

com - ing,　　　you've got me go - ing a - round.　　　Oh, dirt - y

D⁵　C⁵ D⁵　F⁵ G⁵ F⁵　B♭⁵　　C⁵　　　　D⁵　C⁵ D⁵　F⁵ G⁵ F⁵　B♭⁵　C⁵

| ╱ ╱ ╱ ╱ | ╱ ╱ ╱ ╱ | ╱ ╱ ╱ ╱ | ╱ ╱ ╱ ╱ ‖

wom - en,　　　they　don't mess a - round.　　　　　　Let's go!

Interlude

D　Dsus⁴ D　　D⁷　D⁷sus⁴ D⁷　Gmaj⁷　G Gmaj⁷　B♭+　B♭m♭6 B♭+

| ╱ ╱ ╱ ╱ | ╱ ╱ ╱ ╱ | ╱ ╱ ╱ ╱ | ╱ ╱ ╱ ╱ ‖

Bridge

D　Dsus⁴　D　　D⁷　D⁷sus⁴　D⁷　Gmaj⁷　G　Gmaj⁷　B♭+　B♭m♭6 B♭+

‖: ╱ ╱ ╱ ╱ | ╱ ╱ ╱ ╱ | ╱ ╱ ╱ ╱ | ╱ ╱ ╱ ╱ |

　　1. Walk - ing the streets　I won - der, will　it ev - er hap - pen?
　　2. *See additional lyrics*

D　Dsus⁴　D　　D⁷　D⁷sus⁴　D⁷　Gmaj⁷　G　Gmaj⁷　B♭+　B♭m♭6　B♭+

| ╱ ╱ ╱ ╱ | ╱ ╱ ╱ ╱ | ╱ ╱ ╱ ╱ | ╱ ╱ ╱ ╱ :‖

　　Got - ta be good,　'cause ev - 'ry - thing　will be o - kay.

Gtr Solo　　　　　　　　　　　　　　　　　*(repeat and fade)*

D　Dsus⁴　D　　D⁷　D⁷sus⁴　D⁷　Gmaj⁷　G　Gmaj⁷　B♭+　B♭m♭6　B♭+

‖: ╱ ╱ ╱ ╱ | ╱ ╱ ╱ ╱ | ╱ ╱ ╱ ╱ | ╱ ╱ ╱ ╱ :‖

Additional lyrics

Verse
2. The sleepy city is dreaming the nighttime away
　Out on the streets I watch tomorrow becoming today
　I see a man, he's got take-away women for sale
　Yes, for sale
　Guess that's the answer
　'Cause take-away women don't fail

Bridge
2. If I can score tonight then I will end up happy
　A women for sale is gonna help me save my day

ELECTRIC FUNERAL
Words and Music by Frank Iommi, John Osbourne, William Ward and Terence Butler

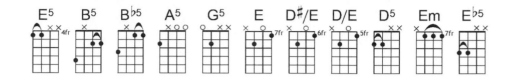

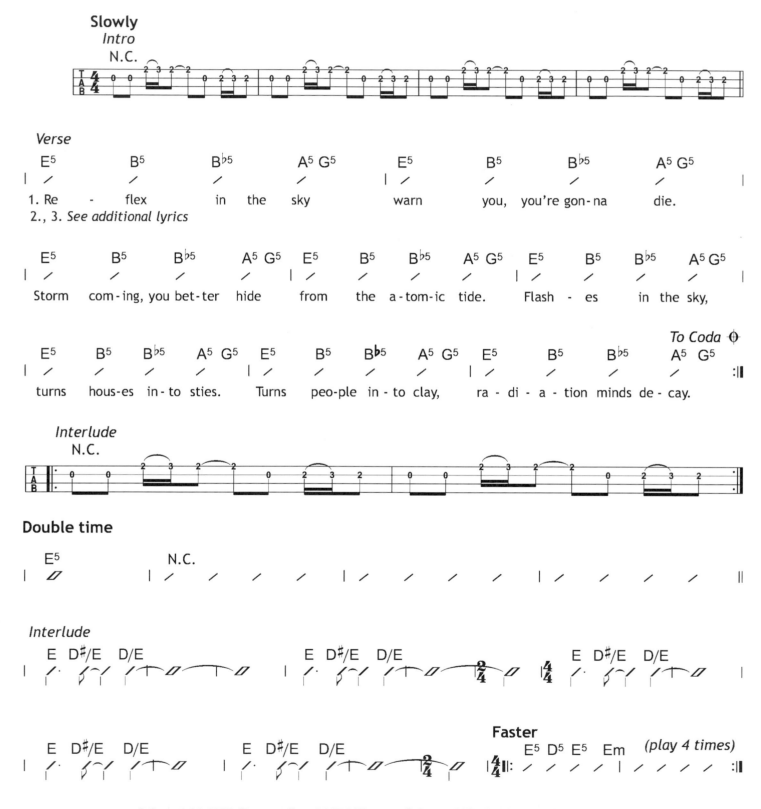

Bridge

N.C.

Build - ings crash - ing down to earth's crack - ing ground.

Riv - ers turned to wood, ice melts in - to blood.

Interlude

E5 D5 E5 Em   E5 D5 E5 Em

N.C.

Earth lies in death bed, clouds cry for the dead.

Ter - ri - fy - ing rain, ease the burn - ing pain.

Chorus

E5 Eb5 D5 B5   E5 Eb5 D5 B5

'Lec - tric fu - ner - al, 'lec - tric fu - ner - al, E -

E5 Eb5 D5 B5   E5 Eb5 D5 B5

lec - tric fu - ner - al, e - lec - tric fu - ner - al.

D5   E5 G5 E5 D5   E5 G5   **Free time** *D.C. al Coda*

Coda

N.C.

(repeat and fade)

E5 B5 Bb5 A5 G5 E5 B5 Bb5 A5 G5

Additional lyrics

2. Robot minds of robot slaves lead men to atomic graves.
   Plastic flowers melt in sun, fading moon falls upon
   Dying world of radiation, victim of man's frustration,
   Burning glow of obscene fire, like electric funeral pyre.

3. And so in the sky shines the electric eye.
   Supernatural King takes Earth under His wing.
   Heaven's golden chorus sings, hell's angels flap their wings.
   Evil souls fall to hell, ever trapped in burning cell.

DIE YOUNG

Words by Ronnie James Dio
Music by Ronnie James Dio, Terence Butler, Anthony Iommi, William Ward

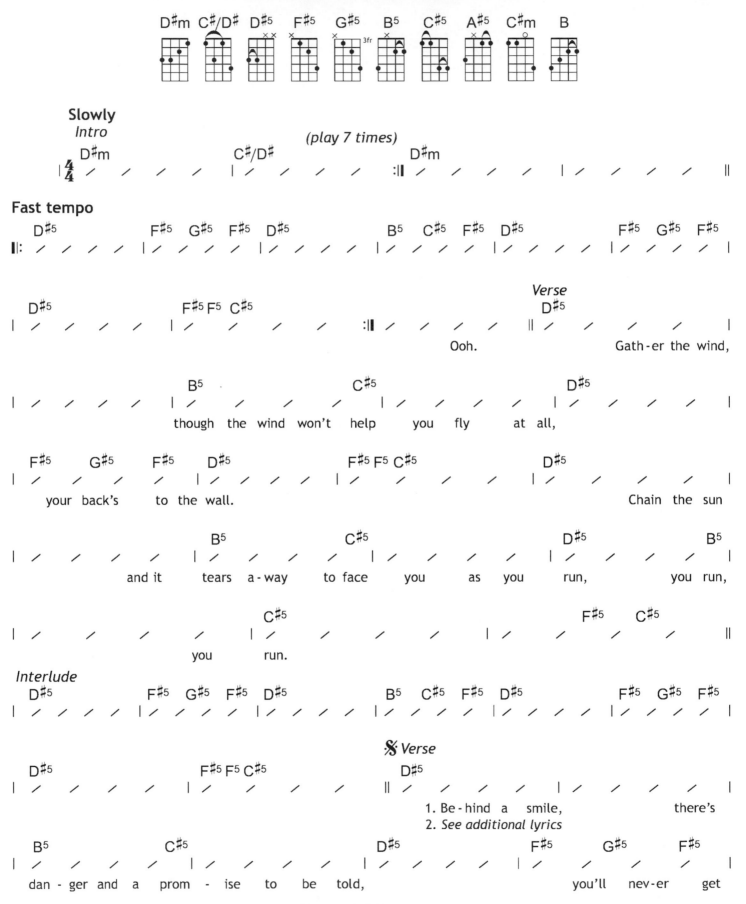

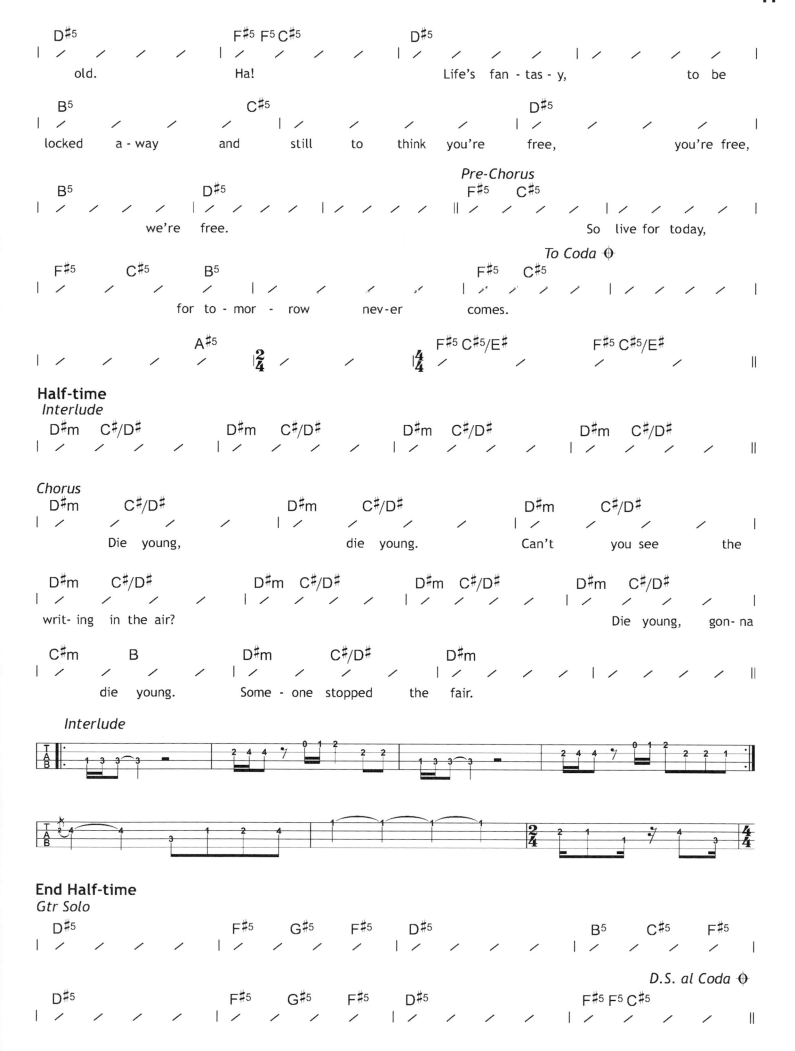

⊕ *Coda*

D#5

| / / / / | / / / / | / / / / | B5 / / / / | C#5 / / / / |

Die   young,   young.   Die

D#5

| / / / / | / / / / | B5 / / / / | C#5 / / / / |

young,   die   young.   Die

D#5

| / / / / | / / / / | B5 / / / / | C#5 / / / / |

young,   die   young,   young.   Die

D#5

| / / / / | / / / / | B5 / / / / | C#5 / / / / |

young,   die   young.   Die   young, die young, die   young, die young, die

D#5

| / / / / | / / / / | B5 / / / / | C#5 / / / / |

young!

(repeat and fade)

D#5

‖: / / / / | / / / / | B5 / / / / | C#5 / / / / :‖

Additional lyrics

2. Gather the wind,
   Though the wind won't help you fly at all,
   Your back's to the wall.
   Then chain the sun
   And it tears away to face you
   As you run, you run, you run.

FAIRIES WEAR BOOTS

**Words and Music by Frank Iommi, John Osbourne,
William Ward and Terence Butler**

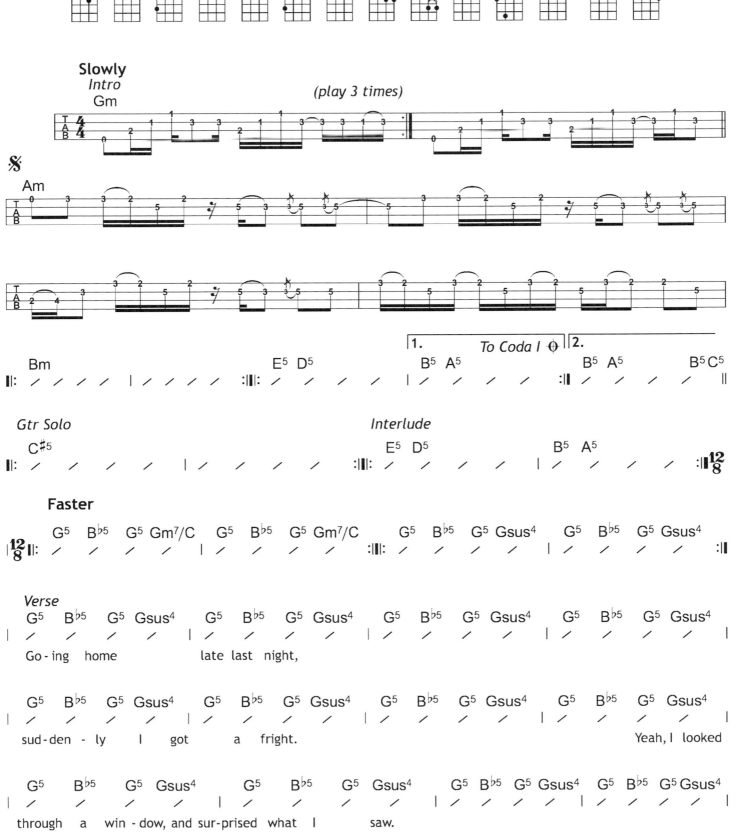

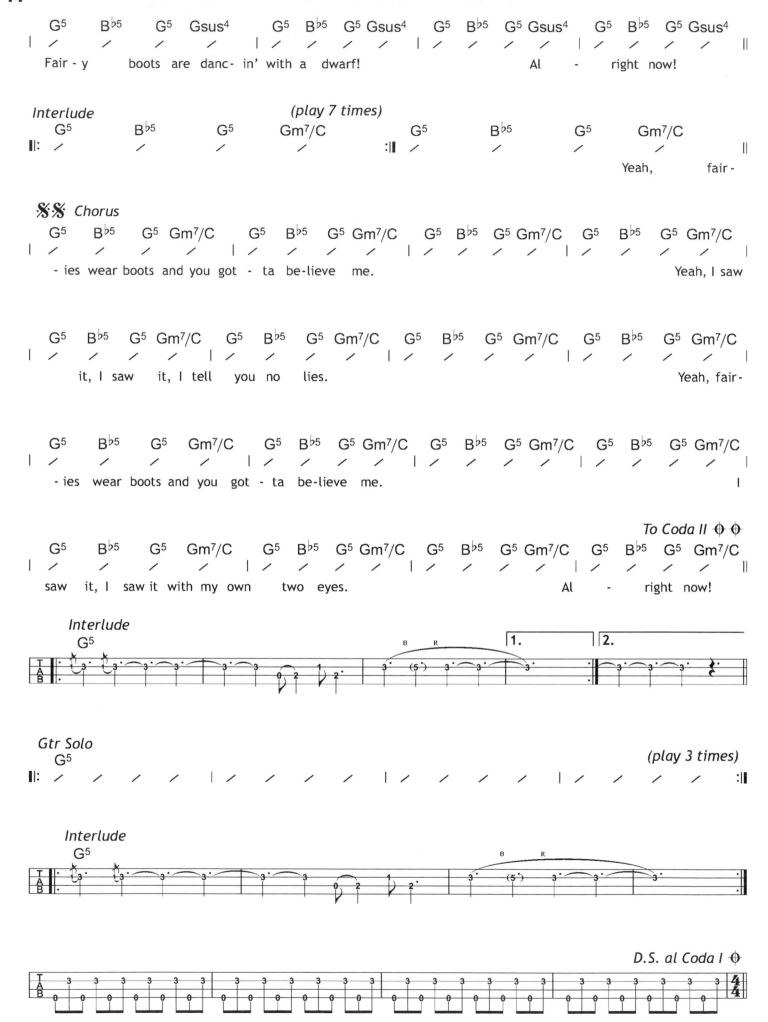

Coda I   **Faster**

E5 D5   B5 A5 $\frac{12}{8}$ G5 B♭5 G5 Gm7/C   G5 B♭5 G5 Gm7/C

1.
G5 B♭5 G5 Gsus4   G5 B♭5 G5 Gsus4

2.   *D.S.S. al Coda II*
G5 B♭5 G5 Gsus4

Yeah, fair-

Coda II

1.
G5 B♭5 G5 Gm7/C   G5 B♭5 G5 Gm7/C

2.
G5 B♭5 G5 Gm7/C

So I went

G5 B♭5 G5 Gm7/C   G5 B♭5 G5 Gm7/C   G5 B♭5 G5 Gm7/C   G5 B♭5 G5 Gm7/C

to the doc - tor see what he could give me.   He said,

G5 B♭5 G5 Gm7/C   G5 B♭5 G5 Gm7/C   G5 B♭5 G5 Gm7/C   G5 B♭5 G5 Gm7/C

"Son,   son, you've gone too far,   'cause smok-

G5 B♭5 G5 Gm7/C   G5 B♭5 G5 Gm7/C   G5 B♭5 G5 Gm7/C   G5 B♭5 G5 Gm7/C

- in' and trip - in' is all that you do."   Yeah!

G5 B♭5 G5 Gm7/C   G5 B♭5 G5 Gm7/C   G5 B♭5 G5 Gm7/C   G5 B♭5 G5 Gm7/C

Outro
G5

(repeat and fade)
G5   F5

HEAVEN AND HELL
Words by Ronnie James Dio
Music by Ronnie James Dio, Terence Butler, Anthony Iommi, William Ward

D#5 E#5 F#5 B5 C#5 G#5 G#m7 C# C#m7 B F# G# C#/E#

Moderately Slowly

Intro

D#5   E#5   F#5   B5   C#5   D#5   E#5   F#5   G#5 F#5 E#5 D#5

D#5

Verse

D#5

1. Sing me a song;   you're a sing - er.   Do me a wrong;   you're a

2., 3. *See additional lyrics*

bring - er of e - vil. The Dev - il is nev - er a mak - er.   The

To Coda

Chorus

B5

less that you give,   you're a tak - er.   So it's   on   and on   and on.

1.

C#5   D#5   D#m   D#5

It's Heav-en and Hell.   Oh,   well.

D#5   D#m   D#5

2. The

2.

C#5   B5   C#5

Oh, it's   on   and on   and on.   It goes

B5   C#5

on   and on   and on.   Heav - en   and Hell.

Interlude (vocal ad lib.)

D#5   E#5   F#5   B5   C#5   D#5   E#5   F#5   G#5 F#5 E#5 D#5

G#m7　　　　　C#　　　　　C#m7　　　　　B　　　　　F#　　　　　C#

| ╱ ╱ ╱ ╱ | ╱ ╱ ╱ ╱ | ╱ ╱ ╱ ╱ | ╱ ╱ ╱ ╱ | ╱ ╱ ╱ ╱ | ╱ ╱ ╱ ╱ |

　　Oh,　　　　　　　　ooh.　　　　　　Yeah, yeah, yeah.

D.S. al Coda

G#　　　　　　　　　D#5　D#m D#5　　　D#5　　D#m D#5

| ╱ ╱ ╱ ╱ | ╱ ╱ ╱ ╱ | ╱ ╱ ╱ ╱ | ╱ ╱ ╱ ╱ | ╱ ╱ ╱ ╱ | ╱ ╱ ╱ ╱ ||

　　　　　　　　　　　　　　　　　　　　　　3. Well if it

Coda　　　　　　　　　　　　　B5　　　　　C#5

| ╱ ╱ ╱ ╱ | ╱ ╱ ╱ ╱ |

　- er.　　　　　And it's　on and on,　　on and on and on,

D#5

| ╱ ╱ ╱ ╱ | ╱ ╱ ╱ ╱ ||

　and on,　and on,　and on,　and on,　and on,　and on,　and on,　and on.

Gtr Solo

D#5　　　　　*(play 7 times)* D#5　　　　D# F# G#m7　　　C#

||: ╱ ╱ ╱ ╱ | ╱ ╱ ╱ ╱ :|| ╱ ╱ ╱ ╱ | ╱ ╱ ╱ ╱ | ╱ ╱ ╱ ╱ | ╱ ╱ ╱ ╱ |

C#m7　　　　　B　　　　　D#5　　　　**Double-time**　　　　*(play 4 times)*

| ╱ ╱ ╱ ╱ | ╱ ╱ ╱ ╱ | ╱ ╱ ╱ ╱ ||: ╱ ╱ ╱ ╱ | ╱ ╱ ╱ ╱ :||

Gtr Solo

D#5　　　　　　　　　　　　C#5

||: ╱ ╱ ╱ ╱ | ╱ ╱ ╱ ╱ | ╱ ╱ ╱ ╱ | ╱ ╱ ╱ ╱ |

F#5　　　　　　　　　　C#5　　　　　1.　　　　　2.

| ╱ ╱ ╱ ╱ | ╱ ╱ ╱ ╱ | ╱ ╱ ╱ ╱ | ╱ ╱ ╱ ╱ :|| ╱ ╱ ╱ ╱ ||

　　　　　　　　　　　　　　　　　　　　　4. They

Verse

D#5　　　　　　　　　　　　　　　C#

||: ╱ ╱ ╱ ╱ | ╱ ╱ ╱ ╱ | ╱ ╱ ╱ ╱ |

(4.) say　that　life's　a　car - ou - sel　spin-ning　fast, you've got to
5. *See additional lyrics*

　　　　　　　　　F#5

| ╱ ╱ ╱ ╱ | ╱ ╱ ╱ ╱ | ╱ ╱ ╱ ╱ |

ride　it well.　The world　is　full　of　kings and queens　who

C#　　　　　　　　　　　　D#5

| ╱ ╱ ╱ ╱ | ╱ ╱ ╱ ╱ | ╱ ╱ ╱ ╱ |

blind　your eyes　then　steal　your dreams. It's　Heav-en and Hell.

1.　　　　　　C#　　　　　　　　　2.

| ╱ ╱ ╱ ╱ | ╱ ╱ ╱ ╱ :|| ╱ ╱ ╱ ╱ |

　Oh, well.　　　　　5. And they'll

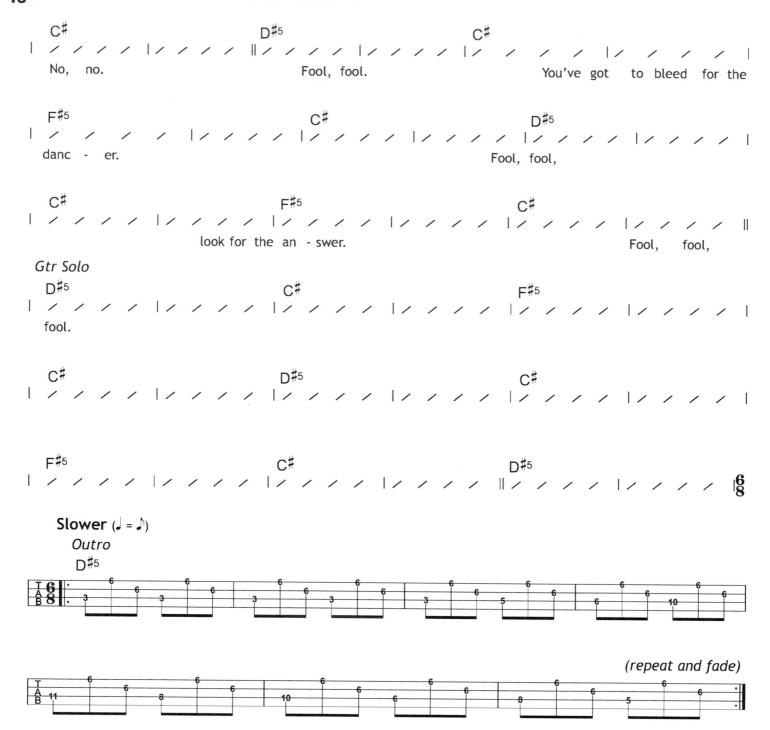

C#
No, no.

D#5
Fool, fool.

C#
You've got to bleed for the

F#5
danc - er.

C#
Fool, fool,

D#5

C#
look for the an - swer.

F#5

C#
Fool, fool,

Gtr Solo

D#5
fool.

C#

F#5

C#

D#5

C#

F#5

C#

D#5

6/8

Slower (♩ = ♪)

Outro

D#5

(repeat and fade)

Additional lyrics

2. The lover of life's not a sinner
   The ending is just a beginner.
   The closer you get to the meaning,
   The sooner you know that you're dreaming.

3. Well if it seems to be real, it's illusion.
   For every moment of truth there's confusion in life.
   Love can be seen as the answer,
   But nobody bleeds for the dancer.

5. And they'll tell you black is really white;
   The moon is just the sun at night;
   And when you walk in golden halls,
   You get to keep the gold that falls.
   It's Heaven and Hell.

IRON MAN

**Words and Music by Frank Iommi, John Osbourne,
William Ward and Terence Butler**

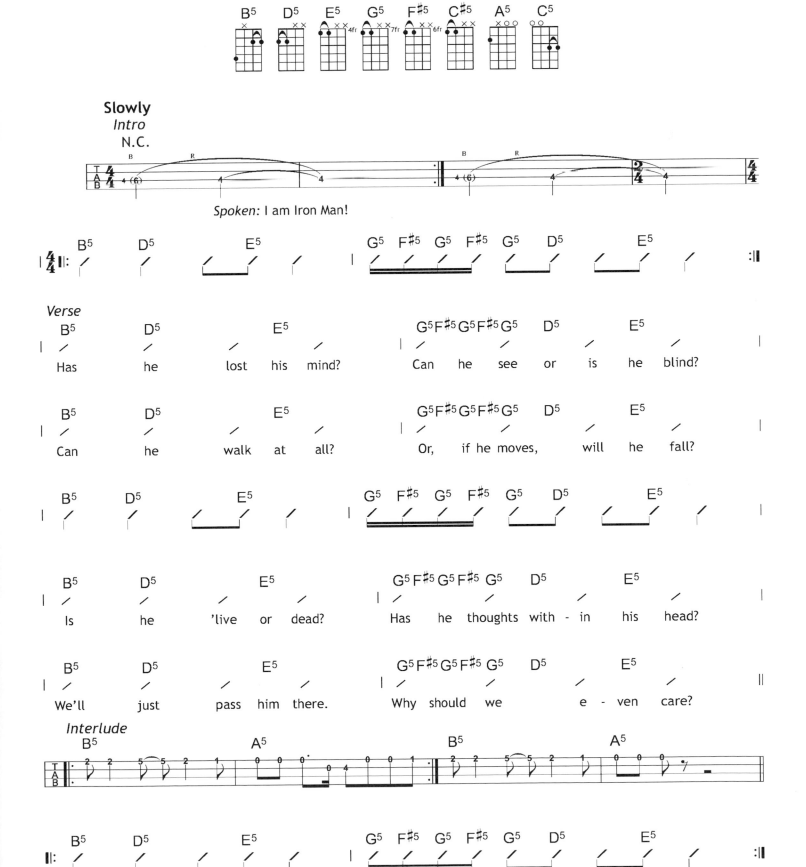

Spoken: I am Iron Man!

Verse

Has he lost his mind? Can he see or is he blind?

Can he walk at all? Or, if he moves, will he fall?

Is he 'live or dead? Has he thoughts with - in his head?

We'll just pass him there. Why should we e - ven care?

Interlude

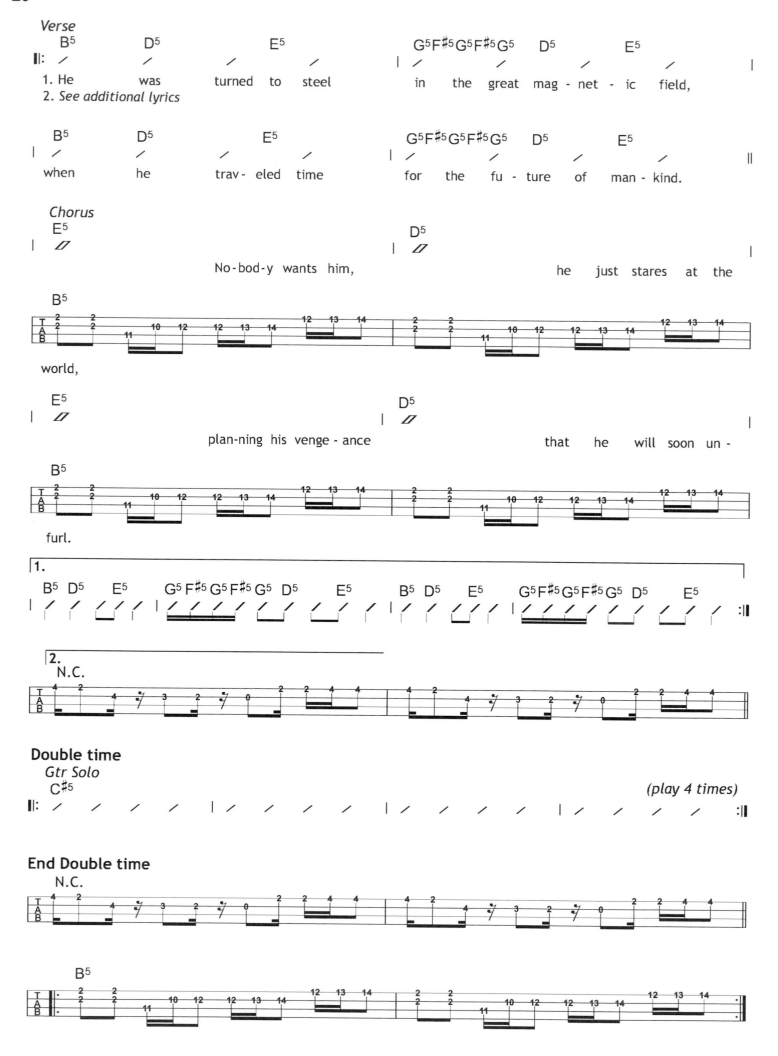

Heav - y   boots   of   lead   fills   his   vic - tims   full   of   dread,

run - ning   as fast as they   can,   I - ron   Man   lives   a - gain!

Additional lyrics

2. Now the time is here
   For Iron Man to spread fear.
   Vengeance from the grave
   Kills the people he once saved.

   Nobody wants him,
   They just turned their heads,
   Nobody helps him,
   Now he'll have his revenge.

LADY EVIL

Words by Ronnie James Dio
Music by Ronnie James Dio, Terence Butler, Anthony Iommi, William Ward

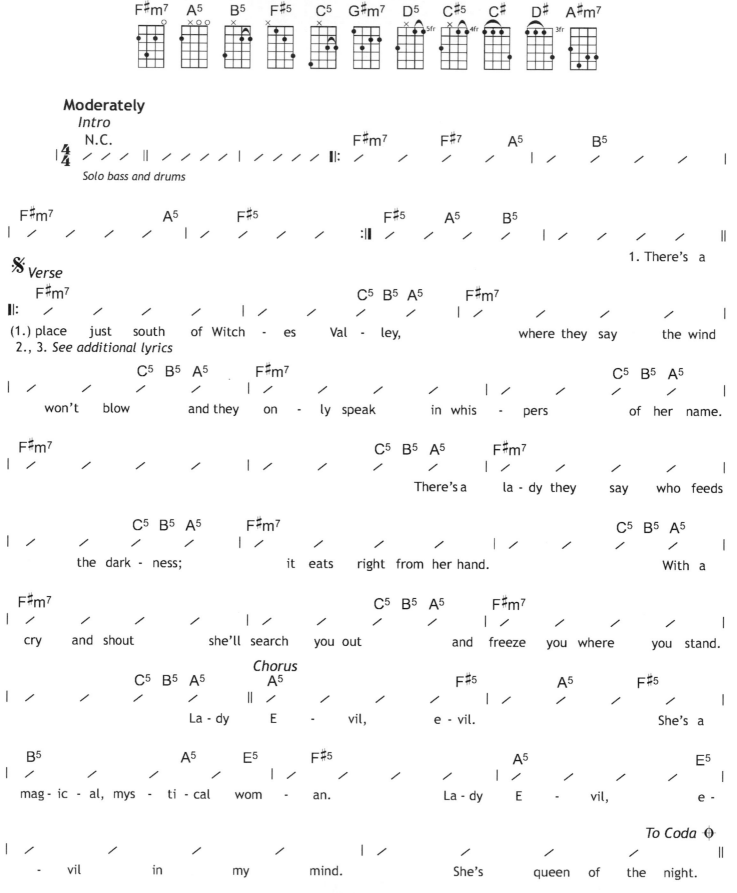

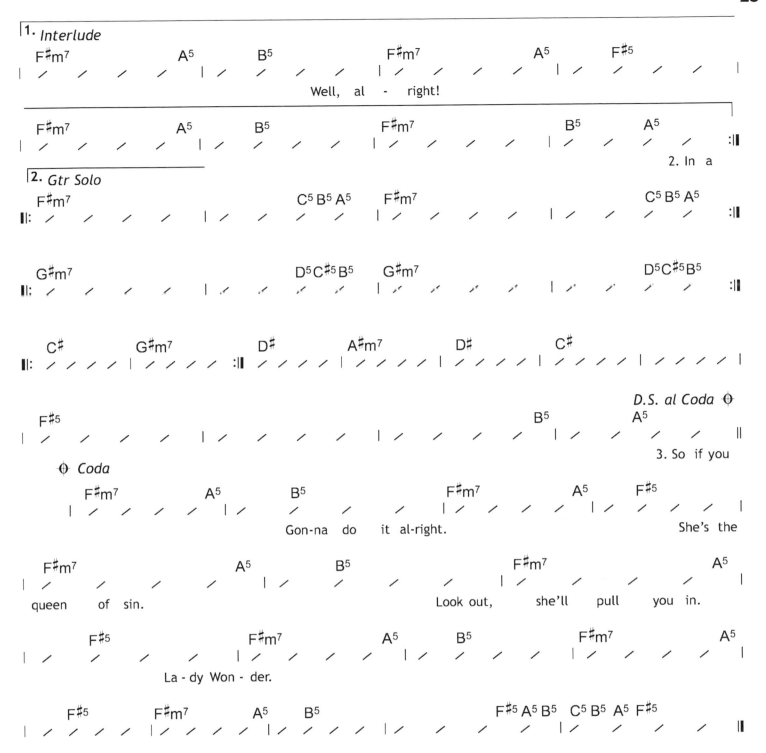

See additional lyrics

2. In a place just south of Witches Valley
   Where they say the rain won't fall
   And thunder cracks the sky and makes it bleed.
   There's a lady they say who needs the darkness;
   She can't face the light.
   With an awful shout, she'll find you out
   And have you before the night.

3. So if you ever get to Witches Valley
   Don't dream or close your eyes
   And never trust your shadow in the dark.
   'Cause there's a lady I know who takes your vision
   And turns it all around.
   The things you see are what you'll be:
   Lost and never found.

LONELY IS THE WORD

Words by Ronnie James Dio
Music by Ronnie James Dio, Terence Butler, Anthony Iommi, William Ward

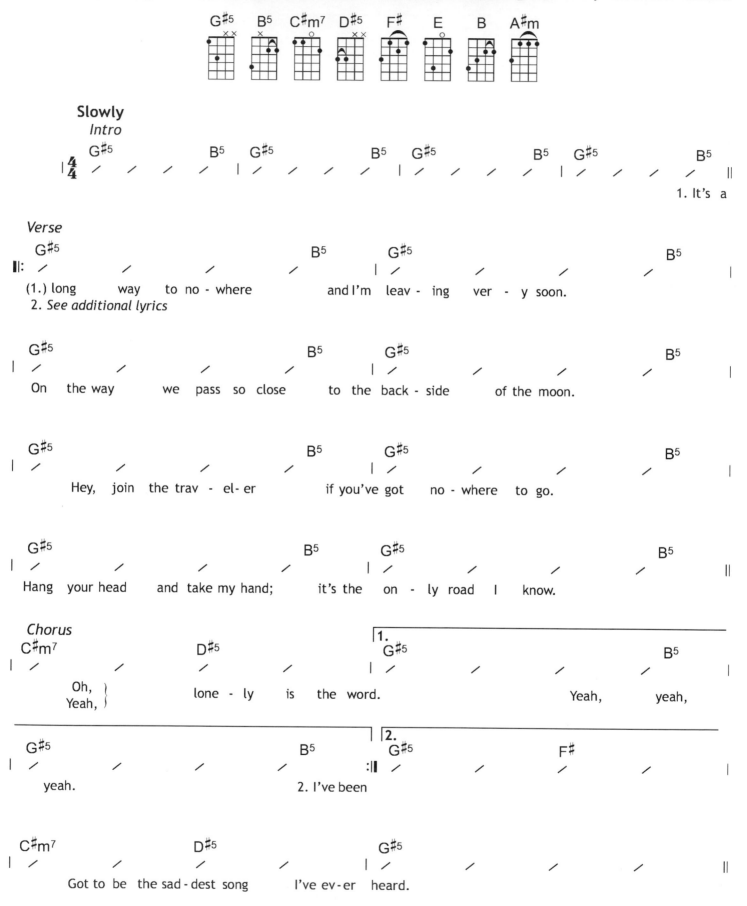

Interlude

G#5   E   *(play 4 times)*   B   A#m   G#5

‖: ╱   ╱   ╱   ╱ | ╱   ╱   ╱   ╱   :‖ ╱   ╱   ╱   ╱ |

Gtr Solo

G#5   E   *(play 4 times)*   B   A#m   G#5   B   A#m   G#5

‖: ╱   ╱   ╱   ╱ | ╱   ╱   ╱   ╱   :‖ ╱   ╱   ╱   ╱ |

C#m7   D#5   G#5   F#   C#m7   D#5   G#5   F#   C#m7   D#5   G#5

| ╱ ╱ ╱ ╱ | ╱ ╱ ╱ ╱ | ╱ ╱ ╱ ╱ | ╱ ╱ ╱ ╱ | ╱ ╱ ╱ ╱ | ╱ ╱ ╱ ╱ ‖

Chorus

C#m7   D#5   G#5   F#

| ╱   ╱ | ╱   ╱ | ╱   ╱ | ╱   ╱ |

Yeah,   lone - ly   is   the   name,

C#m7   D#5   G#5

| ╱   ╱ | ╱   ╱ | ╱   ╱ | ╱   ╱ |

Yeah,   may - be   life's   a   los - ing   game.

Gtr Solo

G#5   E

‖: ╱   ╱   ╱   ╱ | ╱   ╱   ╱   ╱ | ╱   ╱   ╱   ╱ | ╱   ╱   ╱   ╱   :‖

G#5   E   G#5   E   *(repeat and fade)*

‖: ╱   ╱   ╱   ╱ | ╱   ╱   ╱   ╱   :‖

Additional lyrics

2. I've been higher than stardust,
   I've been seen upon the sun.
   I used to count in millions then,
   But now I only count in one.
   Come on, join the traveler
   If you've got nowhere to go.
   Hang your head and take my hand;
   It's the only road I know.

THE MOB RULES

Words by Ronnie James Dio
Music by Ronnie James Dio, Terence Butler, Anthony Iommi, William Ward

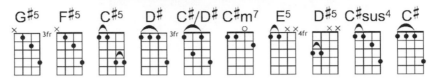

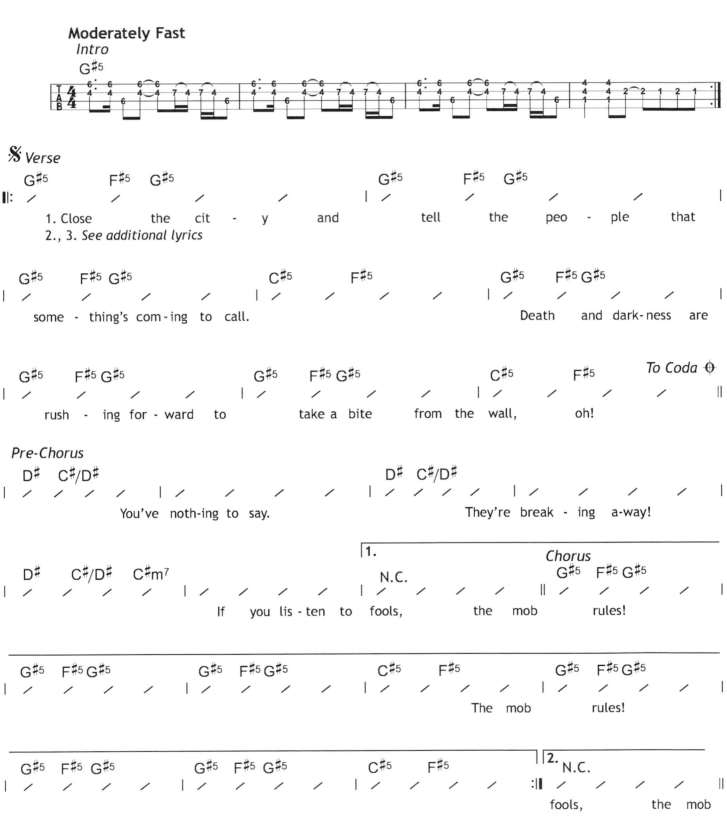

Gtr Solo

C#5 / / / / | / / / / | A5 / / / / | / / / / | B5 / / / / | E5 D#5 E5 D#5 / / / / |

C#5 / / / / | / / / / ‖: C#5 / / / / | / / / / | A5 / / / / | / / / / |

B5 / / / / | E5 D#5 E5 D#5 / / / / | ⌐1. C#5 / / / / | / / / / :‖

⌐2.
Bridge

C#sus4 / C# / / | / / / / | C#sus4 / C# / / |

You've noth‑ing to say. Oh, they're

C#sus4 C# C#m7 / / / | / / / / N.C. / / / / ‖ *D.S. al Coda*

break‑ing a‑way! If you lis‑ten to fools,

Coda
G#5 F#5G#5 / / | G#5 F#5G#5 / / | G#5 F#5G#5 / / | C#5 F#5 / / |

You're all

G#5 F#5G#5 / / | G#5 F#5G#5 / / | G#5 F#5G#5 / / | C#5 F#5 / / |

fools. The mob

G#5 F#5G#5 / / | G#5 F#5G#5 / / | G#5 F#5G#5 / / | C#5 F#5 / / |

rules.

(repeat and fade)
‖: G#5 F#5G#5 / / | G#5 F#5G#5 / / | G#5 F#5G#5 / / | C#5 F#5 / / :‖

Additional lyrics

2. Kill the spirit and you'll be blinded, the end is always the same.
Play with fire, you burn your fingers and lose your hold of the flame, oh!
It's over, it's done, the end is begun.
If you listen to fools, the mob rules!

3. Break the circle and stop the movement,
The wheel is thrown to the ground.
Just remember, it might start rolling and take you right back around!
You're all fools!
The mob rules!

NEON KNIGHTS
Words by Ronnie James Dio
Music by Ronnie James Dio, Terence Butler, Anthony Iommi, William Ward

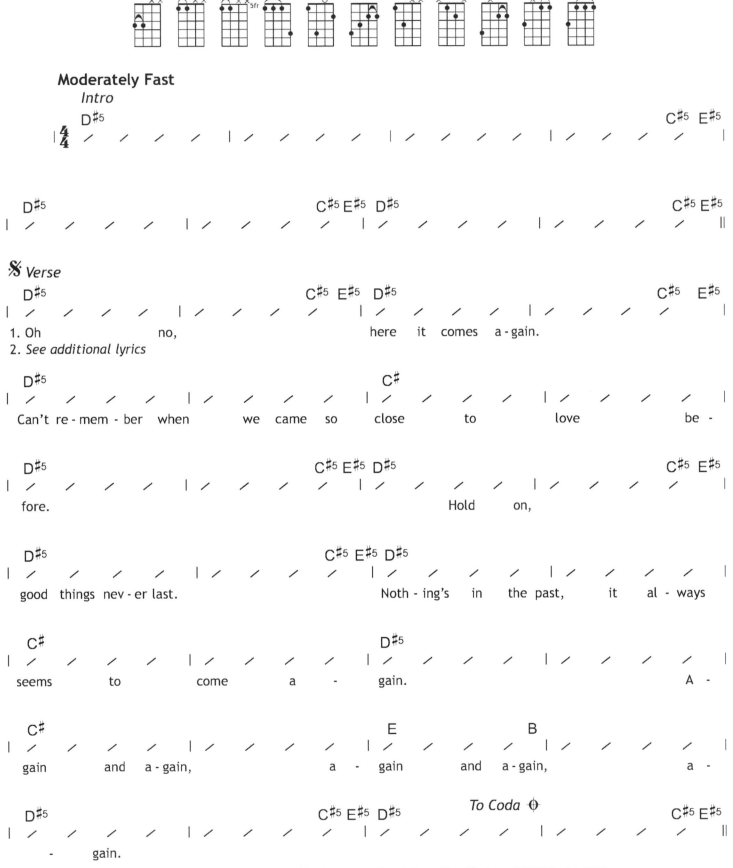

Verse

D#5 | ╱ ╱ ╱ ╱ | ╱ ╱ ╱ ╱ | C#5 E#5 D#5 ╱ ╱ ╱ | ╱ ╱ ╱ ╱ | C#5 E#5

Cry   out   to   le - gions   of   the   brave:

D#5   C#

Time a - gain to save us from the jack - als of the street.

D#5   C#5 E#5 D#5   C#5 E#5

Ride   out,   pro - tec - tors   of   the   realm,

D#5   C#

cap-tains   at   the helm,   sail a - cross   the   sea   of

Pre-Chorus

D#5   G#5   B5   D#5

light.   Cir - cles and   rings,

C#5   B5   G#5   B5   D#5

drag - ons   and   kings.   Weav - ing a charm   and a

C#5   F#5   C#5 D#5 G#5   B5   D#5

spell.   Blessed by the   night,

C#5   B5   G#5   F#5

ho - ly   and   right.   Called   by   the   toll   of   the

Chorus

G#5   C#   B5

bell.   Fly-ing an - gels,   fast de - scend - ing,

C#   B5   G#5

mov-ing on a   nev - er   bend - ing   light.

B5 A#5   G#5   B5 A#5   G#5

C#   B5   C#   B5

Phan - tom fig - ures,   free for-ev - er,   out of shad - ows,   shin - ing ev - er bright.

E   F#5

| / / / / | / / / / | / / / / | / / / / |

Ne - on   knights.

G#5   B5 A#5   G#5   B5   A#5   G#5

| / / / / | / / / / | / / / / | / / / / |

Ne - on   knights.

G#5   B5 A#5   G#5   B5 A#5   G#5

| / / / / | / / / / | / / / / | / / / / ‖

Gtr Solo
D#5   A#m   B5   C#5

‖: / / / / | / / / / | / / / / | / / / / |

(play 4 times)

D#5   G#5   C#5   B5   C#5

| / / / / | / / / / | / / / / | / / / / :‖

D.S. al Coda ⊕

A#5

| / / / / | / / / / | / / / / | / / / / ‖

⊕ *Coda*
             C#5 E#5   D#5   C#5 E#5

| / / / / ‖: / / / / | / / / / :‖

Ne - on   knights.   Ne - on   knights.

D#5   C#5 E#5   D#5

| / / / / | / / / / | / / / / |

All   night.

(repeat and fade)
       C#5 E#5   D#5   C#5 E#5

| / / / / ‖: / / / / | / / / / ‖

Additional lyrics

2. Cry out to legions of the brave:
     Time again to save us from the jackals of the street.
     Ride out, protectors of the realm,
     Captains at the helm, sail across the sea of light.
     Again and again, again and again and again.

N.I.B.

Words and Music by Frank Iommi, Terence Butler, William Ward and John Osbourne

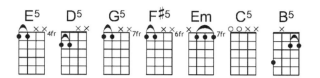

Moderately slowly

solo bass

Oh, yeah!

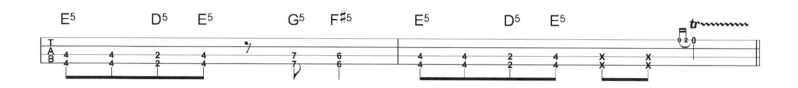

Verse

E5 D5 E5 G5 F#5 E5 D5 E5 Em

Some peo-ple say my love can-not be true.

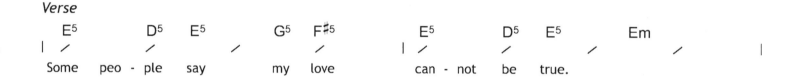

E5 D5 E5 G5 F#5 E5 D5 E5

Please be-lieve me, my love, and I'll show you.

E5 D5 E5 G5 F#5 E5 D5 E5 Em

I will give you those things you thought un-real,

E5 D5 E5 G5 F#5 E5 D5 E5

the sun, the moon, the stars all bear my seal.

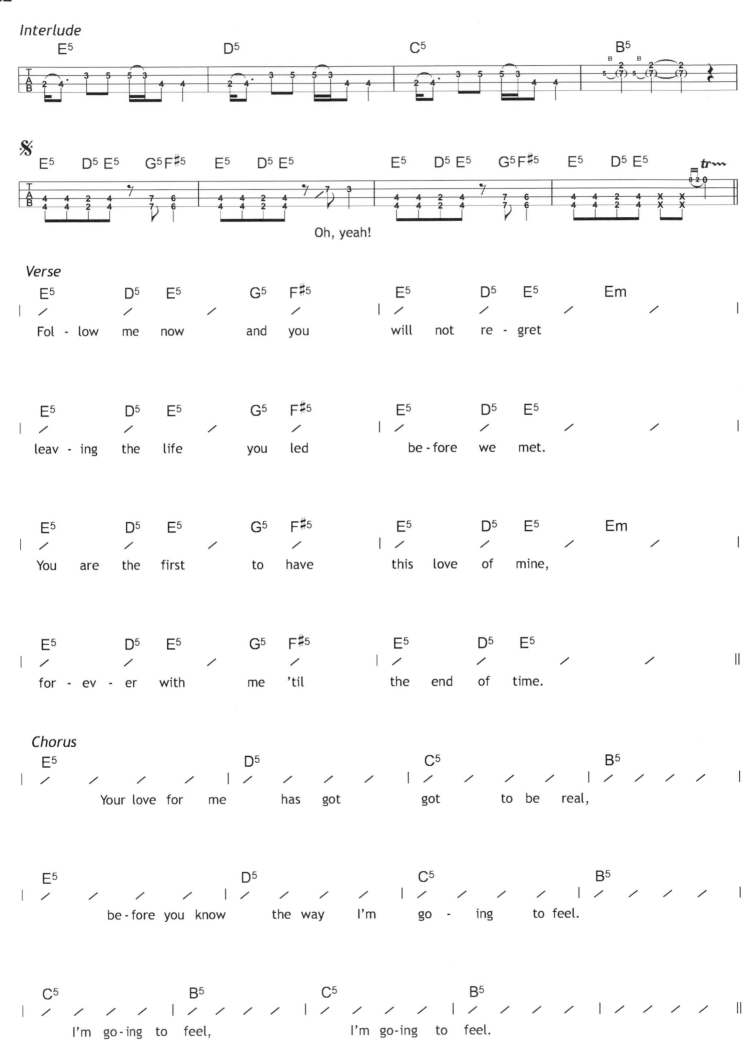

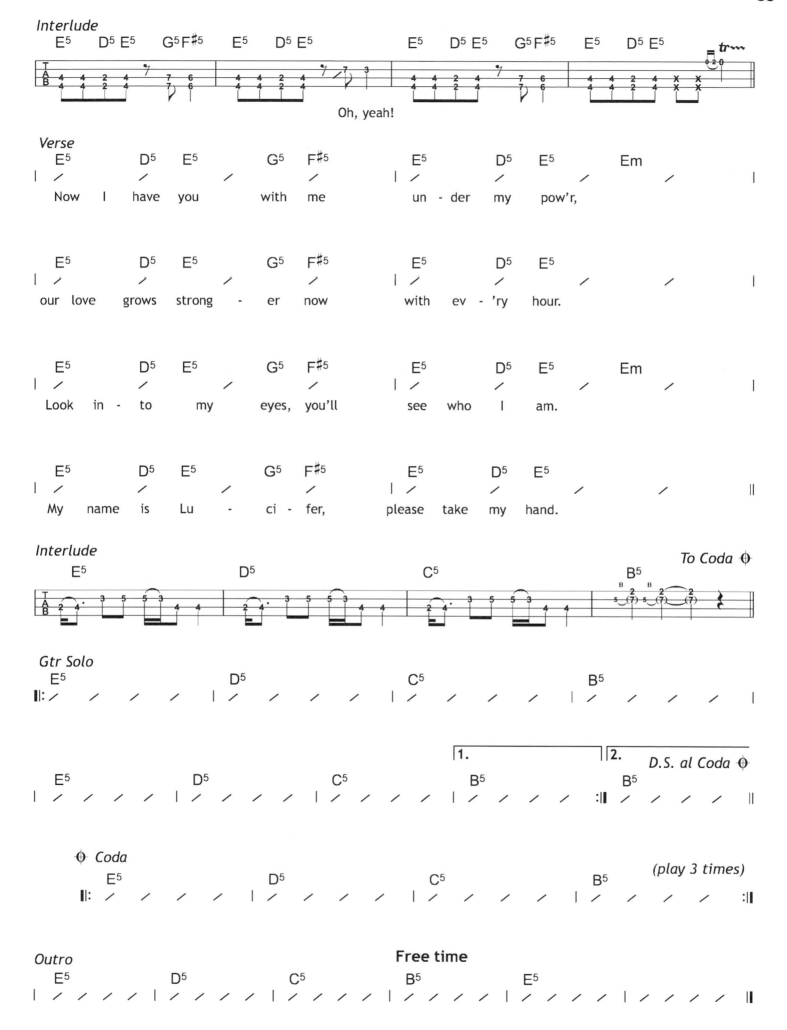

Interlude

Oh, yeah!

Verse

E5 D5 E5 G5 F#5 E5 D5 E5 Em
Now I have you with me un - der my pow'r,

E5 D5 E5 G5 F#5 E5 D5 E5
our love grows strong - er now with ev - 'ry hour.

E5 D5 E5 G5 F#5 E5 D5 E5 Em
Look in - to my eyes, you'll see who I am.

E5 D5 E5 G5 F#5 E5 D5 E5
My name is Lu - ci - fer, please take my hand.

Interlude

To Coda

Gtr Solo

1. 2. D.S. al Coda

Coda
(play 3 times)

Outro Free time

NEVER SAY DIE

Words and Music by Frank Iommi, John Osbourne, William Ward and Terence Butler

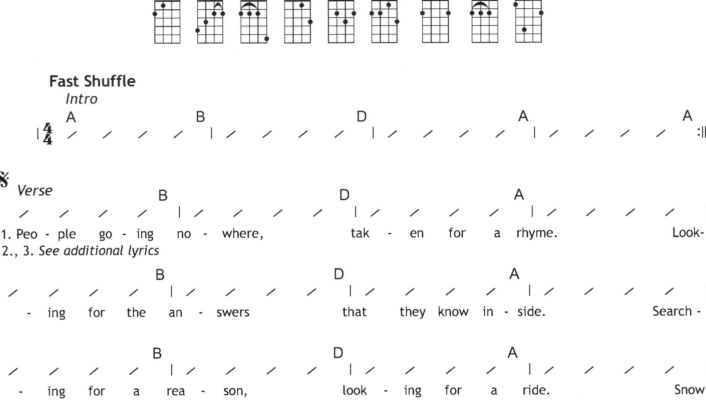

A   B   D   F5   G   Dm7   Am(add9)   D   E

Fast Shuffle

Intro

A   B   D   A   A

$\frac{4}{4}$ / / / / | / / / / | / / / / | / / / / :‖

𝄋 *Verse*

           B   D   A

| / / / / | / / / / | / / / / | / / / / |

1. Peo - ple go - ing no - where,   tak - en for a rhyme.   Look-
2., 3. *See additional lyrics*

           B   D   A

| / / / / | / / / / | / / / / | / / / / |

 - ing for the an - swers   that they know in - side.   Search -

           B   D   A

| / / / / | / / / / | / / / / | / / / / |

 - ing for a rea - son,   look - ing for a ride.   Snow

           B   D   A

| / / / / | / / / / | / / / / | / / / / ‖

White's   mir - ror said,   "Part - ners in crime."

Pre-Chorus

F   A

| / / / / | / / / / | / / / / | / / / / |

Don't they ev - er have to wor - ry?

F   A

| / / / / | / / / / | / / / / | / / / / |

Don't you ev - er won - der why?

F   A

| / / / / | / / / / | / / / / | / / / / ‖

It's the part of me that tells you,   ah,

Chorus

G

| / / / / | / / / / | / / / / | / / / / |

don't you ev - er,   don't ev - er say die.

To Coda ⨁

           A

| / / / / | / / / / | / / / / | / / / / ‖

Nev - er, nev - er,   nev - er say die a - gain.

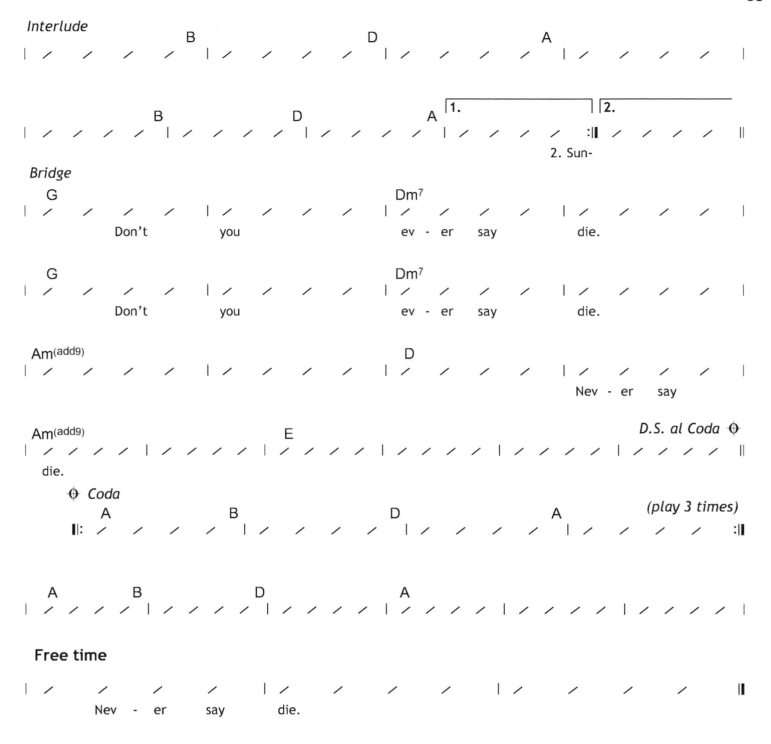

Interlude

Bridge

Free time

Additional lyrics

2. Sunday's satisfaction, Monday's home and dry,
Truth is on the doorstep, welcoming the lies.
All dressed up in sorrow, got no place to go.
Hold tight 'til it's right, takin' it slow.

3. Painted silver lining, writing's on the wall.
Children get together, you can save us all.
Future's on the corner, shoing us the time.
Slow down, turn around, everything's fine.

There's no need to have a reason,
There's no need to wonder why.
It's a part of me that tells you
Oh, don't you ever, don't ever say die.

PARANOID

Words and Music by Anthony Iommi, John Osbourne, William Ward and Terence Butler

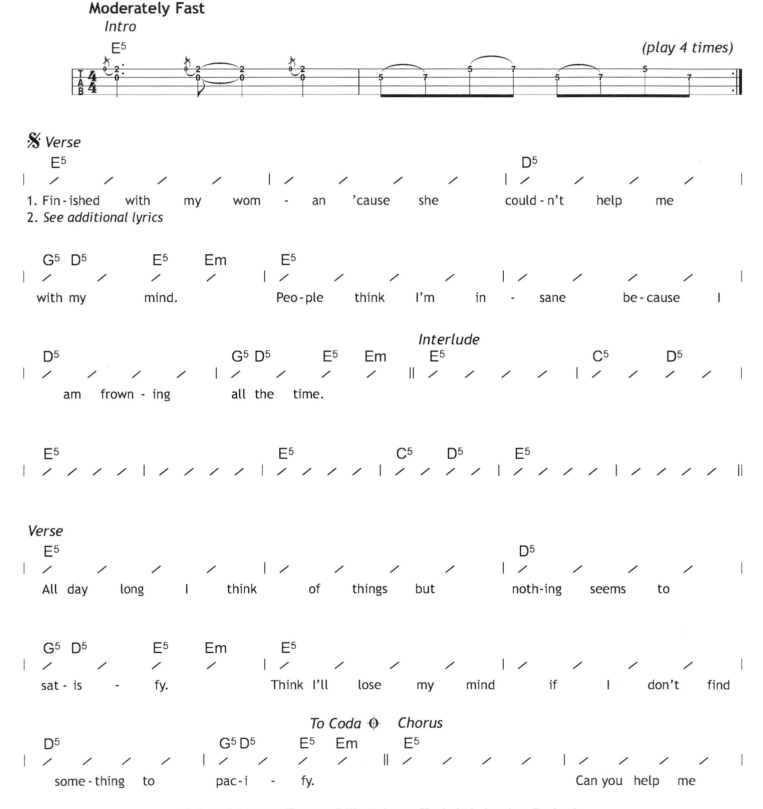

Moderately Fast

Intro — (play 4 times)

Verse

1. Fin - ished   with   my   wom - an   'cause   she   could - n't   help   me
2. *See additional lyrics*

with my   mind.   Peo - ple   think   I'm   in - sane   be - cause   I

am   frown - ing   all   the   time.

Interlude

Verse

All   day   long   I   think   of   things   but   noth - ing   seems   to

sat - is - fy.   Think   I'll   lose   my   mind   if   I   don't   find

To Coda ⊕   *Chorus*

some - thing   to   pac - i - fy.   Can   you   help   me

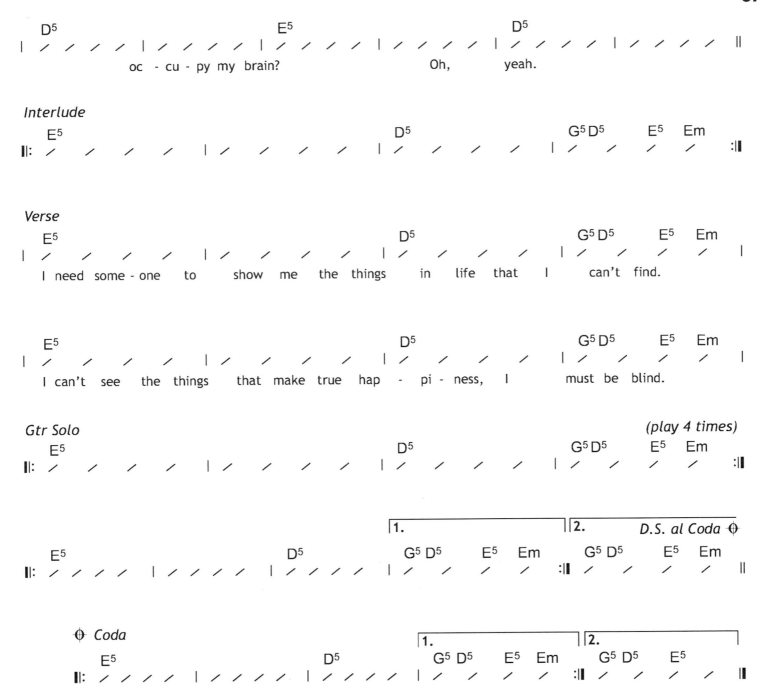

D⁵   E⁵   D⁵

oc - cu - py my brain?   Oh,   yeah.

Interlude

E⁵   D⁵   G⁵ D⁵   E⁵   Em

Verse

E⁵   D⁵   G⁵ D⁵   E⁵   Em

I need some - one to   show me the things   in life that   I   can't find.

E⁵   D⁵   G⁵ D⁵   E⁵   Em

I can't see the things   that make true hap - pi - ness, I   must be blind.

Gtr Solo   *(play 4 times)*

E⁵   D⁵   G⁵ D⁵   E⁵   Em

1.   2.   *D.S. al Coda*

E⁵   D⁵   G⁵ D⁵   E⁵   Em   G⁵ D⁵   E⁵   Em

Coda

E⁵   D⁵   G⁵ D⁵   E⁵   Em   G⁵ D⁵   E⁵

1.   2.

Additional lyrics

2. Make a joke and I will sigh and you will laugh and I will cry.
Happiness I cannot feel and love to me is so unreal.

And so as you hear these words telling you now of my state,
I tell you to enjoy life. I wish I could but it's too late.

SWEET LEAF

Words and Music by Frank Iommi, John Osbourne, William Ward and Terence Butler

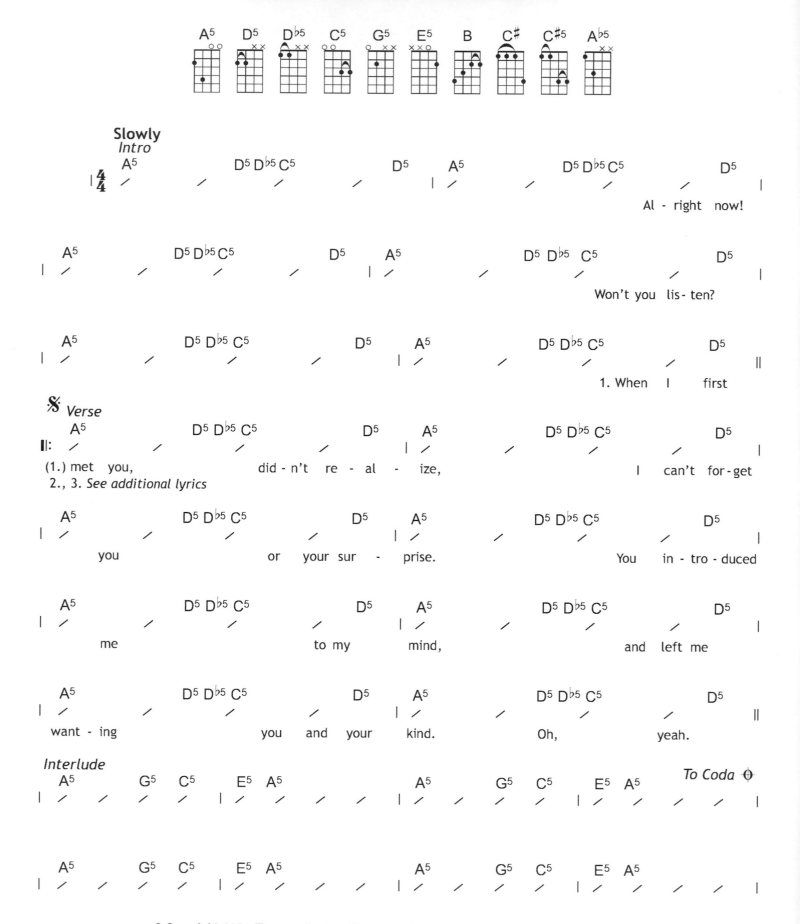

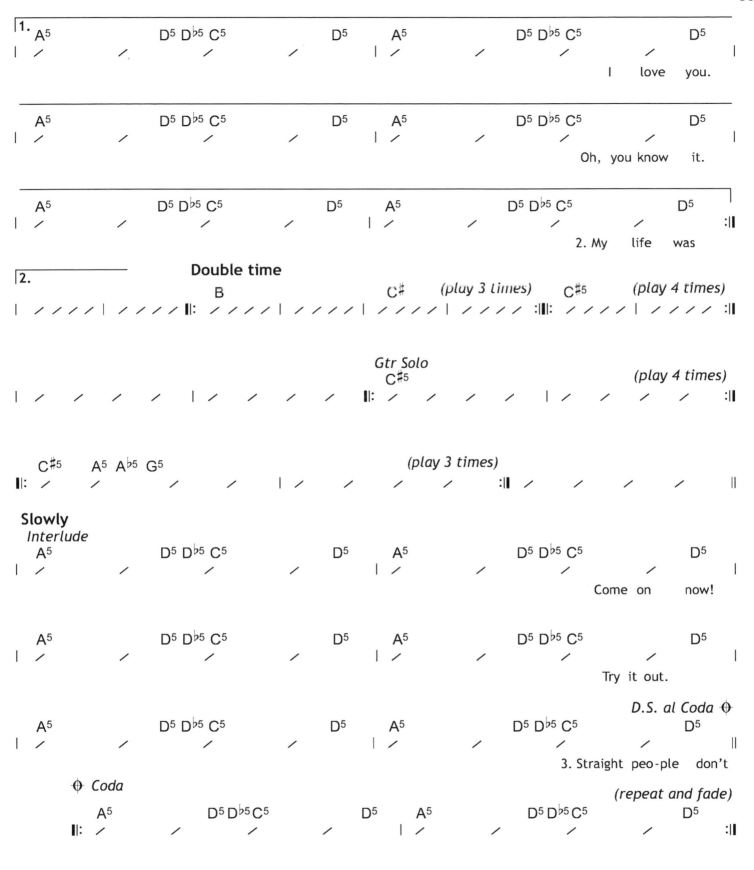

Additional lyrics

2. My life was empty, forever on a down
   Until you took me, showed me around.
   My life is free now, my life is clear,
   I love you, sweet leaf, though you can't hear.
   Oh, yeah!

3. Straight people don't know what you're about,
   They put you down and shut you out.
   You gave to me a new belief,
   And soon the world will love you, sweet leaf.
   Oh, yeah, baby!

SNOWBLIND

**Words and Music by Frank Iommi, Terence Butler,
William Ward and John Osbourne**

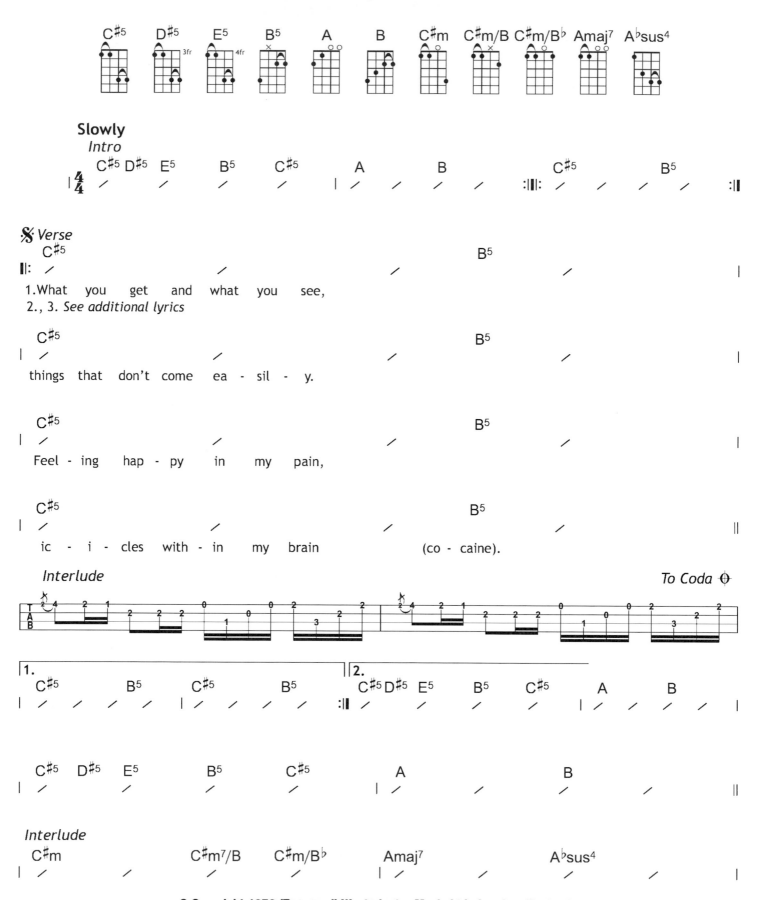

Feel - ing hap - py in my pain,

ic - i - cles with - in my brain (co - caine).

1.What you get and what you see,
2., 3. *See additional lyrics*

things that don't come ea - sil - y.

C#m			C#m7/B	C#m/B♭		Amaj7			A♭sus4		

My eyes   are blind   but I   can   see

C#m			C#m7/B	C#m/B♭		Amaj7			A♭sus4		

the snow - flakes glis - ten on   the   trees.

C#m			C#m7/B	C#m/B♭		Amaj7			A♭sus4		

The sun   no long - er sets   me   free.

C#m			C#m7/B	C#m/B♭		Amaj7			A♭sus4		

I feel   the snow - flakes freez - ing   me.

Gtr Solo   *(play 4 times)*

C#m			C#m7/B	C#m7/B♭		Amaj7			A♭sus4		

Interlude   *D.S. al Coda* ⊕

C#5				B5		C#5			B5		

⊕ *Coda*
Faster

C#5								B5			*(play 4 times)*

12/8

Bridge

C#5						B5					

Don't   you think   I know   what I'm   do - ing,   don't

C#5						B5					

tell   me that   it's do - ing me   wrong.

C#5						B5					

You're   the one   that's real - ly the   los - er,

C#5						B5					

this   is where   I feel   I be - long.   4/4

Slowly

Interlude

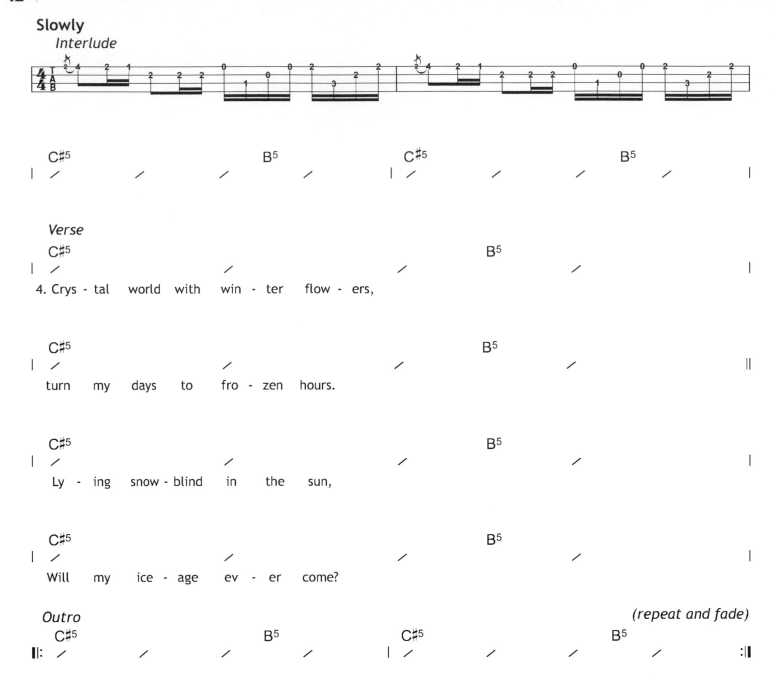

C#5   B5   C#5   B5

Verse

C#5   B5

4. Crys - tal   world   with   win - ter   flow - ers,

C#5   B5

turn   my   days   to   fro - zen   hours.

C#5   B5

Ly - ing   snow - blind   in   the   sun,

C#5   B5

Will   my   ice - age   ev - er   come?

Outro   *(repeat and fade)*

C#5   B5   C#5   B5

Additional lyrics

2. Something blowing in my head,
   Winds of ice that soon will spread,
   Down to freeze my very soul,
   Makes me happy, makes me cold.

3. Let the winter sun shine on,
   Let me feel the frost of dawn,
   Build my dreams on flakes of snow,
   Soon I'll feel the chilling glow.

TURN UP THE NIGHT

Words by Ronnie James Dio
Music by Ronnie James Dio, Terence Butler, Anthony Iommi, William Ward

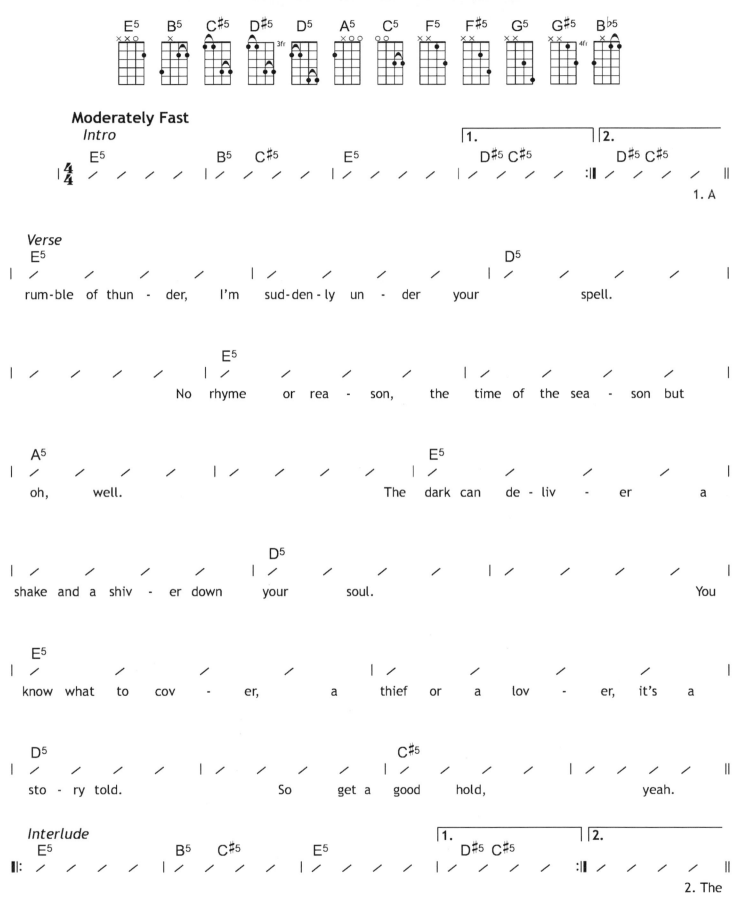

44

𝄋 *Verse*

E⁵ .... D⁵

(2.) rat-tle of voo - doo, you thought that you knew who you are.
3. *See additional lyrics*

E⁵

A sim-ple e-qua - tion, that's the re-la - tion but

A⁵ .... E⁵

that's go-ing too far. A time of sus-pi - cion, a

D⁵

spe-cial con-di - tion that we all know, so let it

C#⁵

all go, yeah! Turn up the night.

Chorus

E⁵ .... B⁵ A⁵ .... E⁵ .... B⁵ A⁵

Turn up the night.

To Coda ⊕

E⁵ .... C#⁵

Turn up the night, it feels so right.

Gtr Solo

‖: E⁵ .... B⁵ .... C#⁵ *Bridge* :‖ E⁵

Night - time sor-

B⁵ .... C#⁵ .... E⁵

- row, tak - en like the pain. Black will not be-come a

B⁵ .... C#⁵ .... E⁵

white, it's all the same. E - vil lurks at twi-

B⁵ .... C#⁵ .... E⁵

- light, danc - es in the dark. Makes you need the move

B⁵ C⁵ C#⁵ D⁵ D#⁵ E⁵ F⁵ F#⁵ G⁵ G#⁵ A⁵ B♭⁵

- ment, like a fire needs a spark to burn!

Gtr Solo

‖: C#5   E5   B5   C#5   F#5 :‖

1. B5   C#5 | **2.** B5   C5   C#5   D5   D#5   E5   F5   F#5   G5   G#5   A5   Bb5 ‖

Interlude

‖: E5   B5   C#5   E5 | **1.** D#5 C#5 :‖ | **2.** *D.S. al Coda* ⊕ D#5 C#5 ‖

3. A

⊕ *Coda*

E5   B5 A5

Got-ta turn up the night.

E5   B5 A5

Turn up the night.   Turn up   the night,

E5   C#5

it feels   so   right.

E5   B5 A5

Turn up the night,   turn up the night,

E5   B5A5   *(play 5 times; vocal ad lib.)*   E5   B5A5   *(repeat and fade)*

get out the light,

Additional lyrics

3. A rumble of thunder,
   I'm suddenly under your spell.
   No rhyme or reason,
   The time of the season but oh, well.
   The dark can deliver a shake and a shiver
   Down your soul,
   So get a good hold!

WAR PIGS

Words and Music by Frank Iommi, John Osbourne, William Ward and Terence Butler

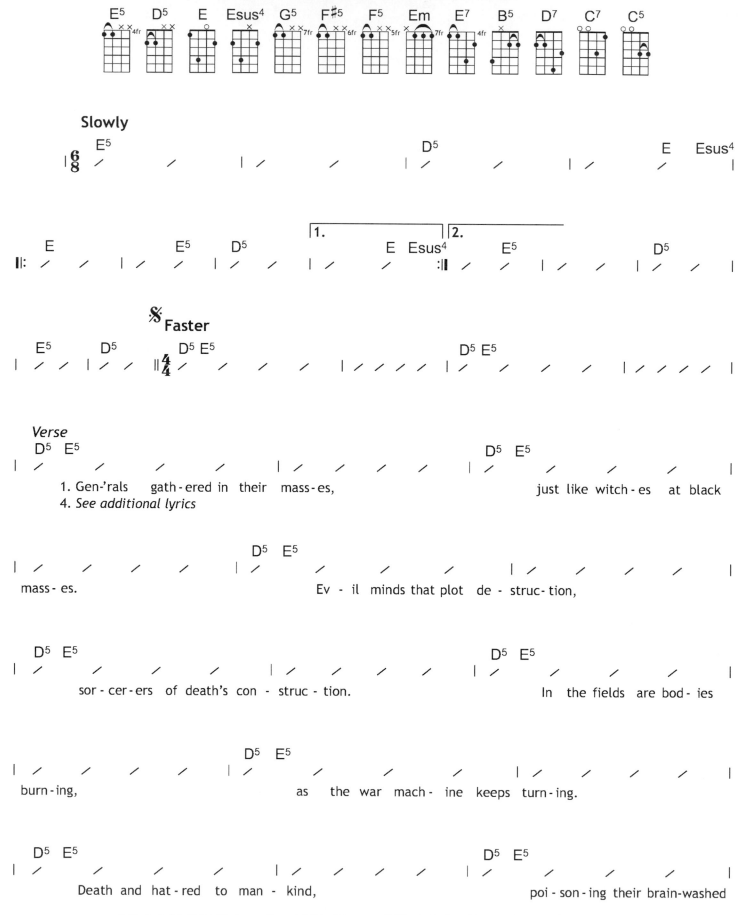

Slowly

§ Faster

Verse

1. Gen-'rals gath-ered in their mass-es, just like witch-es at black
4. *See additional lyrics*

mass-es. Ev-il minds that plot de-struc-tion,

sor-cer-ers of death's con-struc-tion. In the fields are bod-ies

burn-ing, as the war mach-ine keeps turn-ing.

Death and hat-red to man-kind, poi-son-ing their brain-washed

Interlude

D5 E5   G5 F#5 F5   E5   D5 E5   G5 F#5

| / / / / || / / / / | / / / / | / / / / | / / / / |

minds.   Oh, Lord, yeah!

F5   E5   D5 E5   G5 F#5 F5   E5   D5 E5   G5 F#5

| / / / | / / / | / / / / | / / / / | / / / | / / / / | / / / |

To Coda ⊕

F5   E5   E5   Em   E5 G5   E5   Em   E5 G5

| / / / | / / / ||: / / / / | / / / / :||

Verse

E5   G5   E5   G5

||: / / / / | / / / / | / / / / |

2. Pol - i - ti - cians hide them - selves a - way,
3. *See additional lyrics*

E5   G5   E5   G5

| / / / / | / / / / | / / / / |

they on - ly start - ed the war.

E5   G5   E5   G5

| / / / / | / / / / | / / / / |

Why should they go out to fight?

E5   G5   E5   G5

| / / / / | / / / / | / / / / ||

They leave that all to the poor, yeah!

1. *Interlude*

E5 Em E5 G5   E5 Em E5 G5   E5 Em E5 G5   E5 Em E5 G5

| / / / / | / / / / | / / / / | / / / / :||

2. *Interlude*   *(play 4 times)* *Gtr Solo*

D5 E5   G5 F#5 F5   E5   E5

||: / / / / | / / / / :||: / / / / | / / / / :|| / / / / |

E5   *(play 3 times)* *Interlude*
                Esus4 E   E5

||: / / / / | / / / / :|| / / / / | / / / / | / / / / | / / / / | / / / / |

D.S. al Coda ⊕

D5   E5   D5

| / / / / / | / / / / | / / / / ||

𝄌 *Coda*

| E7 | | E7 | | E5 B5 D5 | | E7 | | E5 G5 E5 | |

| E7 | | | | D7 | |

| C7 | | | B5 C5 B5 | |

Gtr Solo

E5 ... D5 ... *(play 8 times)* ... E5 ... D5 ... *(play 4 times)*

Outro

E7 ... D5 E5

Additional lyrics

3. Time will tell on their power minds,
   Making war just for fun
   Treating people just like pawns in chess,
   Wait 'til their judgment day comes. Yeah!

4. Now in darkness, world stops turning,
   Ashes where the bodies burning.
   No more war pigs have the power,
   Hand of God has struck the hour.

   Day of judgment; God is calling.
   On their knees, the war pigs crawling,
   Begging mercies for their sins.
   Satan, laughing, spreads his wings.
   Oh, Lord, yeah!